IT'S MY PARTY!

Complete Plans for Exciting Theme Parties

Laurine Croasdale

and

Carole Davis

Meadowbrook Press

First published in Australasia in 1989 by Simon & Schuster Australia
under the title *Parties! An Ideas and Activities Book for Children*.

© 1989 by Laurine Croasdale and Carole Davis

Published in the United States by Meadowbrook Press, 18318 Minnetonka
Boulevard, Deephaven, Minnesota 55391.

Publisher's ISBN: 0-88166-137-6

BOOK TRADE DISTRIBUTION by Simon & Schuster, a division of Simon and
Schuster, Inc., 1230 Avenue of the Americas, New York, New York 10020.

Simon & Schuster Ordering #: 0-671-70781-7

90 91 92 93 94 5 4 3 2 1

Designed by Deborah Brash/Brash Design
Typeset in Avant Garde by Post Typesetters
Produced by Mandarin Offset
Printed and Bound in Hong Kong

Contents

Acknowledgments 6

Introduction 7

Planning the Party 8

Castaways 10

Ghosts, Ghouls and Phantoms 16

Cave-Dwellers 20

Come as a Spy 24

The Enchanted Garden 30

Space Station Zero 34

The Big Top 38

Basic Recipes 44

Materials 47

Acknowledgments

The authors would like to thank the following people for their interest and encouragement during the preparation of this book: Michele Ford, Chris Sayer, Katharine and Tim Gerrard, Zara the Fortune Teller, Bad Joke Johnny, Beastie and Monster Marel Sr., Deb Brash, Rosalind and Bill Cumines, Deidre Hardy, Jayne Denshire, Claire Craig and all other willing party goers and throwers.

Special thanks to Margaret Connolly, Mike Sloane, Simon Davis and Steve Hand for their enthusiasm and support.

I would like to dedicate this book to my mother who encouraged and allowed me to explore the world of fantasy.

Carole Davis

This book is for all children under 100 who love a good party.

Laurine Croasdale

Introduction

They all arrived at once — a colorful huddle of tightrope walkers in tutus, strong men with painted mustaches, and clowns in dad's baggy trousers — all clutching their entry tickets to the Big Top. Zara the Fortune Teller greeted them at the door and the Ring Master led them to the Big Top where the face painter had paints at hand. It didn't matter that the costumes were homemade or the decorations hastily concocted, the party was a big hit anyway.

It's My Party! is a compilation of party dress, games and decoration ideas presented in seven themes for children from ages five to ten. The book works on a number of levels — it is a range of party and activity suggestions that parents can adapt to suit their time, budget and available space as well as a children's picture and activity book. It is extremely unlikely that any parent would hold a party and include all the suggestions given, yet they might want to select a few decorations, get costume ideas using things from around the home or use the suggestions as a base for their own ideas. When testing out the ideas in this book we gave parents different themes to follow for their child's party. Seeing the ideas at work was very rewarding, as each parent utilized a few of the ideas and added some of their own to create a little extra excitement for a special person.

Explained throughout with colorful illustrations, the book weaves from one party to the next, opening the scene for each theme with a cast of characters who tell the reader what the party is about, how to dress the part, games to play and decorations and special food to make. Many of the decorations and costumes are simple yet effective and can be made by the children themselves or with a little parent supervision. The emphasis is on simplicity and nearly all items in the book can be made from recycled home materials or inexpensive paper products available from local shops. It may be that the next party is a long way away, but to fill in a rainy day, children can use one of the ideas for a play theme, adapt costumes from their own clothes and create their own games.

It doesn't take a lot of effort to transform your child's party into a novel and fun event — just a few ideas, a little planning and lots of enthusiasm.

Carole Davis and Laurine Croasdale

Pardon us but we are trying to find the party that's around here!

Planning the Party

There are no specific rules and guidelines to organizing a party for your child that will guarantee a successful day. On trying out the parties in this book, we discovered that, even with the same themes, every party took on its own character according to the children, the locale and the ideas each parent used.

By the same token we found that parents' situations varied enormously with time and/or money restrictions, but all wanted to buy or prepare something to make their child's birthday a special occasion. For this reason we have included as many ideas as possible so that the parent with little time can select just a few ideas to make or adapt by buying a similar substitute. Parents with a small party budget can make decorations using the suggested recycled materials or inexpensive paper products, and those with lots of energy may want to spend time with their children, making some of the more involved decorations. There are no shoulds and shouldn'ts; it's a case of adapting the book to suit yourself. As well as being a special day for your child, it has to be fun (and manageable) for you too.

Here are a few observations we made along the way that you may find helpful. Start by making an outline of the kind of party that is realistic for you to hold: who would your child like to invite, what is a sensible time, which party suits an indoor/outdoor setting and can be quickly organized, when is it convenient to hold the party, what is your budget, how much space do you have? Keep it simple yet spontaneous and work within your own boundaries.

Party Basics

A manageable size for a party tends to be around twelve to fifteen children, unless you have a lot of space. An optimum length is around one and a half to a maximum of two hours. Try to hold the party when most children can attend. If the birthday falls during school holidays for example, hold it a week or so beforehand. Organize the party at a convenient time, such as midafternoon, especially if young children are involved. If it's likely the party will be held indoors, consider hiring a magician or juggler. They normally perform for around twenty to thirty minutes and are well worth the fee.

Choose an area in the home that suits the selected theme and that is large enough for the number of children invited. Each party has been listed according to whether it works best in an indoor or outdoor setting. A decorated garage creates the best atmosphere for a Space Station Zero or Come as a Spy party, a darkened room suits the Ghost party, while a garden is the best setting for the Cave Dwellers or Enchanted Garden party. If the weather rules out use of the garden look at the garage, playroom or sunroom as an alternative location. If you only have a small area, choose a theme that will adapt to the space and concentrate on games that don't require much activity.

If the weather is unpredictable, prepare a back-up area equipped with materials and toys where the children can play. Provide table mats or name cards to decorate, modeling clay to make jewelery, or theme items and a dress-up box with additional things to wear.

Invitations

An invitation with a little pizzaz can add much to the party. The children's excitement on receiving it, and their anticipation, all add to the enjoyment of the event. Include your child's full name, phone number, address and a map (if the place is difficult to find). It is also important to include a starting and finishing time for parents' information. Each party includes an invitation that is easy to enlarge on a photocopier, fill in and send out.

Family Involvement

Children's parties are a great opportunity for the whole family to join in the fun, especially if you get involved in dressing up and making decorations. Before the party, encourage your child/

children to start collecting items for decorations and costumes, and a week before, plan an afternoon for making decorations and trying on costumes. Aim to have all preparation done well before the party starts so you feel more relaxed and can enjoy the time with the children.

Arrivals

Often children arrive at a party and suddenly feel shy or anxious about their parent leaving. To overcome this, plan some kind of activity such as drawing on a graffiti board or making simple hats; specific suggestions are included with each party. Also, keep a few simple costume pieces at the door, such as hats or sashes, in case a child arrives without a costume.

Decorations and Costumes

Many of the decorations and costumes in the book are straightforward and can be made by the children themselves using their own clothing or items that can often be found around the house. The emphasis is on simplicity and color with specific ideas and instructions for each party. Listed with each party is a collection of relevant things that can be gathered to make a costume along with illustrations showing how they can be put together. These ideas do not have to be used, they are suggestions for you to choose from and adapt according to what you can lay your hands on. A materials list on page 47 suggests items that can be collected for recycling into costumes or decorations.

Games

The games suit two different age groups and include both indoor and outdoor activities. Generally outdoor parties tend to work without much direction, so the emphasis has been placed on either indoor games or games that easily adapt to a confined space. Games can also be mixed from party to party simply by adapting the game to fit the theme.

Food

A menu of food suggestions is included with each party and a section of tested recipes can be found on page 44. These suggestions are intended to be supplements to the usual favorites that children expect. Finger food that doesn't need cutting and can be eaten easily tends to be the most suitable. If space allows, set up a table for the children to eat at and cover it with a decorated, disposable tablecloth. To minimize your cleaning up, set the table with paper plates and cups that can be rolled into the cloth at the end and thrown out.

Ask any child what they like about parties and chances are you won't get them past 'The Cake'. The thicker the icing, the better the party! So don't worry if you aren't a great cake baker, just make şure it's colorful. We have included only two cake recipes, a basic cake and a chocolate cake, which may be baked in different shapes and decorated to suit the theme.

Prizes/Going Home Bags

A little treat for each child to take home is a great way to round off the party, and children have assured us that age does not diminish their enjoyment of this final treat. Keep the gift small, and to avoid any squabbles, give each child the same present. In addition, buy a selection of small prizes to give away during the party. Again these should be small gifts, but make sure that each child wins something and is not left out. A pass-the-parcel game is always good to hold last, just in case any child has missed out.

CASTAWAYS

Castaway Clothes

Cannibal Chief

Bones, feathers, straw skirt, spear, body paint

Jetsam

Strips of cellophane and crepe paper seaweed, shells, bottle tops, feathers, crabs… in fact anything you might find washed up on the beach

Castaway

Tattered straw hat, shell necklace, torn jeans

Hula Girl

Flowers, paper lei (see illustration page 12), straw skirt, bikini top, shell jewelery

Beachcomber

Old shirt tied at waist, cut off jeans, sneakers, big straw hat, sack full of beach stuff, pockets full of shells

Snorkeler

Swimsuit, mask, snorkel, flippers, seaweed, spear with fish

S.O.S!

I'm shipwrecked on a desert island at

_____

and am inviting fellow castaways to celebrate my ___ th birthday on _____ at _____ until _____

P.S. Bring your swimsuit, you may have to walk the plank. Catering by The Sharkeaters Arms.

R.S.V.P. _____

Roll up the invitations and put them into plastic bottles to deliver them.

To decorate your invitations:

Draw and color your own "ocean" map on the reverse of the invitations, then ask an adult to dampen the edges and burn them slightly with a candle.

Central Avenue Sea

Cliff St. Straits

Neighborhood Lagoon

Making Your Island...

Shells, palm leaves, flowers, balloons, cardboard boxes for canoes, lobsters made from toilet paper rolls and pipe cleaners, crabs from plastic tops and pipe cleaners, fish mobile, paper butterflies, blue or green tarpaulin for lagoon.

Palm Trees

You will need: big cardboard tubes, cardboard, scissors, glue, sticky tape, balloons, paint, paintbrush, string, bucket. Place palm tree in bucket and fill with sand.

PAINT

Seagull Border

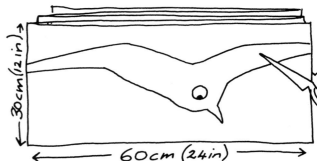

30cm (12in)

60cm (24in)

You will need: a roll of brown paper or newsprint, a pencil, scissors, and an orange and a black marker pen.

Fish Mobiles

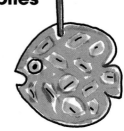

Draw different-shaped fish on pieces of cardboard, paint both sides in bright colors with patterns. Hang them from trees, doorways or ceiling.

IDEA

Give each guest a crepe paper "lei" as they arrive.

Paper Lei

You will need: crepe paper scissors strong thread large needle

Cut into 5cm (2in) strips.

Make sure thread is long enough to fit easily over the head.

Run scissors down edges to "frill."

Stitch with running stitch and pull tightly.

When thread is nearly full spiral, twist the paper and tie off securely.

Games

Pin the Tail on the Seahorse

Draw a seahorse on a large sheet of paper, then cut out and color the tail. Each child is blindfolded, gently turned around three times and then given the tail to pin on the seahorse. The child who pins the tail closest to the seahorse wins a prize.

Pass the Fish

Wrap up a prize in lots of newspaper, old wrapping paper and brown paper in the shape of a fish. The children sit in a circle and pass the parcel from one to the other while music is played. When the music stops, the child holding the parcel unwraps a layer. The child who gets to unwrap the last layer wins the prize.

Not fish again!

Sharks and Fish

Have the children (the fish) standing at one end of the garden and three selected children (the sharks) sitting around the garden. When someone calls out "Sharks love to eat little fish" the fish have to swim across the garden without being tagged by one of the sharks, who can only move about on the spot. If a fish is tagged it becomes a shark. The last fish left is the winner.

Captain Blood's Treasure

Captain Blood stands at one end of the room facing the wall with his treasure behind him. The other pirates creep toward Captain Blood on tip-toe from the opposite end of the room. If Captain Blood looks around the pirates must freeze. If they are seen moving they must go back to the wall and start again. When close enough to the treasure, the pirates must grab it and run back to the start. If Captain Blood catches them, a new game begins and the thief becomes Captain Blood.

Sea Bed Shuffle

Divide the children into two teams lined up behind the starting line. When the parent calls out "Crabs," each child at the front of their team moves sideways like a crab toward the finish line. The winner scores a point for their team. When the parent calls "Jellyfish," the next child in each team races to the finish, wobbling and slithering, just like a jellyfish all the way. Keep on calling until all of the children have a turn.
Make a list of various sea creatures whose movements can be easily imitated, such as lobster, snapping turtle, sea snake, shark, etc. The team with the most points wins.

Yummy!

The Sharkeaters Arms Menu

Green Lagoon page 44

Dugout Canoes *

Coral Reefs * page 45

The Fish Bowl*

Shipwreck Salad with Thousand Island Dressing

Fish Cookies page 44

Tropical Fruit Salad *

Jaws Jell-O* and Coconut Ice Cream

Plantation Punch

Island Cake * page 46

Chocolate coins to take home

* see illustrations

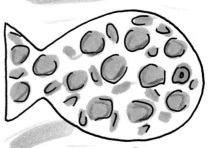

Play Hawaiian music at your party!

Tropical Fruit Salad

Prepare fresh fruit. To prevent fruit discoloring, toss it in lemon juice. Make the salad the morning of the party and chill it well. Garnish with mint leaves and serve with ice cream.

Serve in half melon shell.

Coral Reefs

Arrange around the edge of Lagoon Dip.

Plantation Punch

1 large can pineapple juice
pineapple chunks
large bottle ginger ale
orange segments
ice cubes

Serve in a hollowed-out pineapple or a large jug. Mix just before serving.

Jaws Jell-O

Cut oranges with sharp knife, break in half and use the pulp in the fruit salad.

Pour Jell-O in each one and use sprinkles left over from cake to decorate.

The Fish Bowl

Serve candy fish and shells from a goldfish bowl. The fish bowl can also be a centerpiece for the party table.

Dugouts

Remove some of the bread from fresh sesame rolls and fill with: chicken and avocado, ham and pineapple, and egg salad. Put children's names on flags.

Scott

Jamie

Island Cake

Crumbs!

Simon

Going home bag

brown paper

string

sticky tape

20cm (8in)

15cm (6in)

Fold

Peter

Dress and Misbehavior

Vampires

Long black cloak, white shirt, bow tie, black pants, pointy shoes, white face, red lipstick, long sharp teeth, slicked back hair, blood dribbles, member of blood bank badge, black nail polish, very polite, hate the daylight, always look for bare necks, avoid people who eat garlic, never look in the mirror

Phantoms

Body suit with mask, cloak, hoods, torch, phantoms have a habit of appearing silently out of nowhere

Zombies

Green body paint, filthy clothes, bare feet, unbrushed hair, walk slowly, stare straight ahead, smell of the grave, deadpan face, fluorescent paint on clothing to give eerie glow (don't use it on your skin)

Ghosts

White sheets, gauze, pillow cases, painted rubber gloves, torch under face, chains to rattle, move silently but prone to sudden groans

Mummies

Strips of old sheet, bandages, safety pins, musty smell, Egyptian jewelery, mummies are always lost

Skeletons

White face with black makeup, black body suit, white bones painted on suit, bone rattle, skeletons sneak up on people and rattle their bones loudly

Invitation

Come at night and give us a fright.

_____

is invited to a haunting

on ——— from — to ———

at _____

_____

R.S.V.P. ———

food from:
Tombstone Takeouts

Decorations

Encourage webs, send the cleaner on a very long vacation!!

Make paper chains, buy cobwebs at the local magic shop, paint balloons as ghouls, make pipe-cleaner spiders, put colored cellophane over lights.

bat border

25cm(10in)
20cm 8in
pencil
fold
black paint

Plastic or paper bags

HERE SITS
- - - - - - -
BORN

Paint your own balloons.

ghost mobile

Stop the clock with the hands at midnight.

IDEA

GAMES

Bat-a-cake

Ghost Busters

Make up a series of ghostly clues and give each child the first clue, such as, at "Midnight" you will find your next clue. Place the other clues around the house and yard for the children to follow. The first child to find all the clues wins a prize.

Ghost Story (turn lights off, shadow screen in one corner)

The children sit in a circle. A parent begins a story something like this: "Suddenly the rain stopped. The wind grew stronger, howling around the tombstones. The moon edged behind a cloud, and in the distance a hooded rider on horseback approached." The first child in the circle then tells part of the story, the next child tells a bit more, and so on around the circle until each child has told a part of the story. A parent can also tell a story while someone acts out the story behind the shadow screen.

Graveyard Grab

One child is blindfolded and counts to ten while the others hide in the yard or room. The child then goes hunting for the others who have to get back to base unseen. If they are caught they swap places with the child who was blindfolded.

Rattling Chains

Before the party, tape a variety of noises: chains, squeaks, creaking doors, tapping, dripping water. List all the sounds and give them a number. Play the tape in a darkened room. The children have to guess the sounds, and the one with the most correct answers wins.

Shadow Play

Hang a sheet across the corner of the room and stand a strong lamp in the corner directed at the sheet. The children are each given a card and when their name is called they stand behind the sheet and act out the instructions on the card, such as the ghoul rose from the grave, dracula flew forth, the blood bank is closed ... while the other children guess what they are doing.

Tombstone Takeouts Menu

White with Fright Dip page 45

Scream of Tomato Soup

Eyeballs*

Devilled Fingers

Staked Sausages*

Dem Bones page 45

Batwings page 44

Spook Salad

Skull Cookies * page 44

Dracula Jell-O * with Shocklate Ice Cream

Cobweb Cake * page 46

Midnight Madness

Candy worms to take home*

* see illustrations

YUK!

Eyeballs

jelly bean

large marshmallow

Midnight Madness

Set blood drops (red jelly beans) into ice cubes, then mix with lime drink mix, cherries and soda, just before serving.

Dracula Jell-O

red Jell-o

plastic fly

Staked Sausages

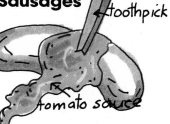

toothpick

tomato sauce

Skull Cookies

white icing

black icing or licorice shapes

Candy Worms

Pass another eyeball please.

Have you been eating garlic?

No! I always smell like it!

Fluoride has stopped decay

My Daddy is a Pharoah.

No kidding? Mine's a hood.

What's the matter, has the cook got your tongue?

Cobweb Cake

IDEA

Use an old sheet spattered with red paint for the tablecloth.

CAVE DWELLERS
Next thing you know, man will be trying this!
Does anyone know a good dentist?
Let's rock, O.K.?

Cave Fashion Trends

- best shaggy bath mat (uncombed)
- old towels
- pillow case tunics
- fake fur rugs
- rag rug, off the shoulder
- grandma's old fox fur
- leopard-spotted bathrobe
- teased, mud-dressed hair
- wigs/beards
- charcoal smudged face
- reddish-brown makeup
- bone jewelery*
- leather thonging (bootlaces)
- polished bones, hand carried
- bottle club*

* see illustrations

 —Give each guest a charcoal smudge as they arrive.

Tablecloth

Decorate a paper tablecloth with prints of your own hand, foot or your pet's paw dipped in poster paint.

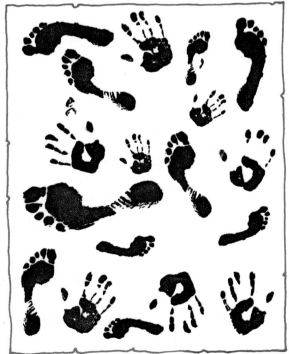

 Just when were lightbulbs invented?

Cave Dwellers & Trogs
Come to my cave at

_____

on _____ between _____
to celebrate my
____ th birthday

Bring your favorite rock for Pet Rock of the Year Competition.
Catering by The Bedrock Cafe.
RSVP _____

Bone Jewelery

Collect small bones for several weeks before your party. Boil them well, then bleach them in the sun. Collect string, leather strips, pieces of old fur (not off your cat) and even small, bleached driftwood pieces from the beach. Tie the bones and other items onto the leather or string and make a necklace. If you can't collect these pieces, make your own shapes with modeling clay.

Bottle Clubs

Glue two or three layers of small, torn pieces of paper all over a large, plastic soft drink bottle. Let paper dry thoroughly, then paint in suitable colors. Clear varnish will make the club last longer.

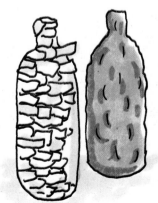

Games

Club Golf

Paint plastic drink containers in bright colors and attach them to sticks to make clubs. Set up some painted cardboard boxes around the room or yard to make a mini golf course. Use ping pong balls as golf balls and tap them with the clubs into the cardboard boxes. The player who completes the course with the lowest number of shots is the winner.

Trog's Treasure

Seat the children in a circle. The trog sits in the middle of the circle with eyes closed, guarding a treasure between its feet. The children in the circle try to steal the treasure without the trog hearing them. If the trog hears a noise, it may open its eyes and catch the thief. The successful thief gets to be the trog.

Reptile Wriggle

All players hold hands and form a long line, then the child at one end leads the line into a spiral, winding around the child on the other end. When the spiral is complete, the head child gets down on hands and knees and crawls out through everyone's legs. Everyone in the line must follow without dropping hands.

Sauropod's Tail

Divide the children into two groups. One group forms a circle. The other group makes up the sauropod by lining up and grasping the child in front around the waist. The sauropod moves around in the circle while the children in the circle try to tag the last child in the sauropod. When that child is tagged, the tagger goes to the front of the sauropod and the tagged child joins the circle.

Rolling Stones

Collect several smooth, round stones. Then make hoops to roll them through by cutting sections of wire or hose, shaping them into semi circles and sticking them into the ground. Divide the children into two teams and give each child a few stones. Play some music to time each team. The team that can roll the most stones through the hoops while the music is playing is the winner. For variety, set up a selection of other obstacles to roll the stones through.

This is taking pets too far!

The Bedrock Cafe Menu

Dinosaur Dip page 44

Barbecued Diptrodon Ribs page 44

Brontoburgers*

Pterodactyl Wings page 44

Sabre Tooth Salad

Club Sandwiches

Rock Cakes page 44

Trog's Toenails page 44

Stegosaurus Thickshakes

Ice Age Blocks*

Gigantosaurus Cake* page 45

Fossil Fudge to take home*

* see illustrations

Brontoburger

You will need: sesame buns, lettuce, cheese, tomato slices, ketchup, mayonnaise, ground beef patty.

Fossil Fudge

Make fudge (page 45). When fudge is nearly set, but still warm, cut into "fossils" using a very small, shaped cookie cutter.

Stegosaurus Thickshakes

Mix in blender:
ice blocks
yogurt
honey
fresh fruit
milk
fruit juice

Serve freshly made.

Ice Age Blocks

Freeze candy dinosaurs inside lemonade popsicles.

Gigantosaurus Cake

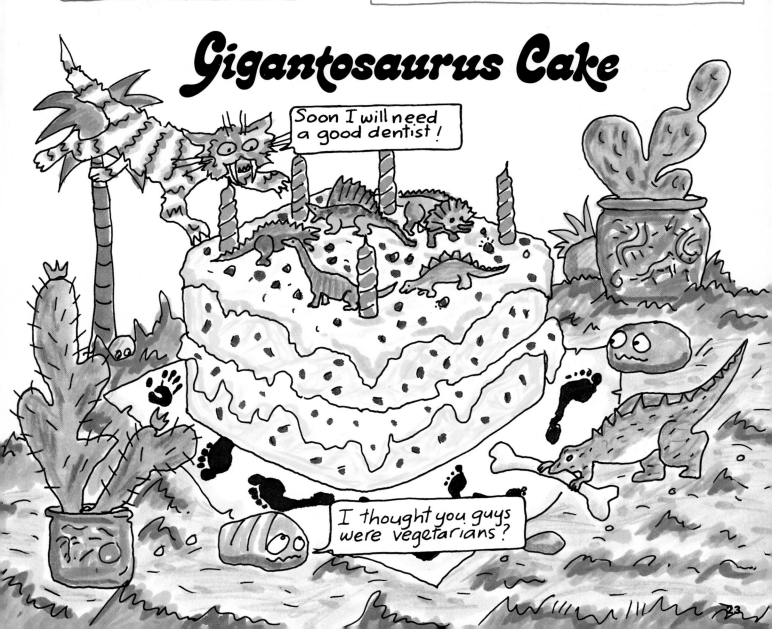

Soon I will need a good dentist!

I thought you guys were vegetarians?

SPOTTED IN ALL HEADQUARTERS

- garage set up as headquarters
- spy books
- water pistols
- cardboard refrigerator box
- metal detector
- desk
- typewriter
- telephone
- single light bulb
- filing cabinet
- magnifying glass
- pack of cards
- coat hooks
- map on wall
- secret escape plans
- fingerprint pad
- wanted posters
- red tape
- shredded computer paper
- waste paper basket
- torches
- paper, pens and pencils
- "bugs"
- periscopes*
- string telephones*
- walkie talkies*
- binoculars
- tape recorder

* see illustrations page 27

WANTED! ALL SPIES

THE CHIEF ALIAS..................
COMMANDS THE PRESENCE OF
.........................ALIAS NO.........
AT HQ ....
ON ....
AT ....UNTIL ....

DRESS IN DISGUISE

**YOUR FIRST MISSION STARTS ON ARRIVAL.
RATIONS BY KGB KATERING.**

Send a copy of spy code with invitation.

Secret seal your envelope by dripping melted candle wax onto it and then scratching in a secret sign before the wax sets.

Carry a loud ticking clock in your bag!

WANTED

MOSCOW MIKE

WANTED

SHADY SHIRLEY

WANTED

DICK THE DAGGER
(ALIAS CARL THE CLOAK)

DISGUISES

- hats
- overcoats
- gloves
- veil
- cloak
- ski mask
- false noses
- mustaches
- soft-soled shoes
- sunglasses
- disguise kit and make up
- notebook and pen
- handkerchief
  (for wiping prints)
- torch
- mirror
- binoculars
- umbrella
- personal stereo
- camera
- brief case

SPY'S CODE

All the best spies in spy movies follow this code. If you want to be a spy, follow the code too. Remember to wear your number at the party.

1. Always be on time
2. Always be in disguise
3. Do not divulge your name, only answer to your number
4. Always carry the correct papers — your invitation and ID card
5. Never leave fingerprints — wear gloves or wipe surfaces
6. Always have a reason for being somewhere
7. Be on the alert for double agents
8. Don't leave any evidence
9. Do not get caught on a mission
10. Always keep the chief's name a secret

I told you to keep it under your hat!

String Telephone

You will need:

2 clean tin cans   hammer
ball of string   large nail
2 matchsticks

Using the hammer and nail, make a hole in the bottom of each can. Thread string through and secure with matchsticks.

Walkie Talkie

You will need:

milk cartons
knitting needles
buttons
toothpaste tops
glue
paint
sticky tape

Periscope

You will need:

long box
2 mirrors
glue
scissors

Ask an adult to help you to make this.

MISSION POSSIBLE

SECRET MISSION FOR AGENT . . . .

TAKE A CAN OF FOOD AND HIDE IT IN THE MAILBOX

Signed

SECRET MISSION FOR AGENT . . . .

TAKE A BOOK FROM THE SHELF AND PUT IT IN THE BROOM CLOSET

Signed

SECRET MISSION FOR AGENT . . . .

CHANGE THE SOCKS ON THE CLOTHESLINE WITH YOUR OWN

Signed

SECRET MISSION FOR AGENT . . . .

CHANGE YOUR DISGUISE

Signed

Post the tooth to the end of the line.

Post the tooth to mend the line.

Spy Catcher

With the invitation each spy receives a copy of the Spy's Code and a badge or card with a number on it. Each spy follows the code at the party and the best spy receives a prize.

Mission Impossible

As the guests arrive at the party, give each one a small envelope containing a mission, such as those on page 27. All spies have to complete their missions some time during the party.

Past the truth to the end of the line.

Post the tooth to mend a lie.

Spy Ring

All spies sit in a circle. The Chief whispers a sentence into the ear of the first spy who then passes it on to the next spy. The code is passed around the circle until it gets back to the Chief. The last spy to receive the code repeats the message and then the Chief tells the original one.

Mind Bender

Put a selection of small objects, such as marbles, buttons, spoons, sharpeners, etc., into a cloth bag or toilet bag. Each spy can feel the objects in the bag for 60 seconds and then write down what is inside. The spy with the highest number of correct items wins.

Pass the truth to the end of the line.

Past the tooth to Mandalay?

Taste Interrogation

Each spy, in turn, is blindfolded while the other spies give him tidbits of food to taste, such as cubes of cheese, apple, grapes, olives, nuts, etc. The spy who correctly guesses the most pieces of food is the winner.

What put you onto my scent?

KGB KATERER'S MENU

Devious Dip page 45
Double Agents (double
 sandwiches)
Mission Rations
Undercover Pizza page 45
Suspect Salad
Clue Cookies*
Bugged Jell-O* with ice cream
Eastern Blocks (red colored
 ice blocks)
Truth juice*
Bomb Cake* page 46
Furtive Fudge to
 take home page 45

* see illustrations

It's all lies!

Truth Juice

1 can crushed pineapple
1 large can pineapple juice
1 large bottle ginger ale
ice cubes

Mix just before serving.

Bugged Jell-O

plastic "bug"

Mission Rations

1 candy bar
2 dried apricots
1 pkt Lifesavers

Wrap in silver foil and
identify with agent's number.

While fudge is
still warm, mark
into squares and
put a thumbprint
on each one.

IDEA

Clue Cookies

Make cookie recipe (page 44).
Cut into squares, bake, then ice
part of a word onto each one.
Spies match words before
eating them.

hand   cuff
foot   print
sus   pect

Bomb Cake

← Candle

silver
sprinkles

chocolate
icing

piped
icing

I knew I
was on the
right track.

29

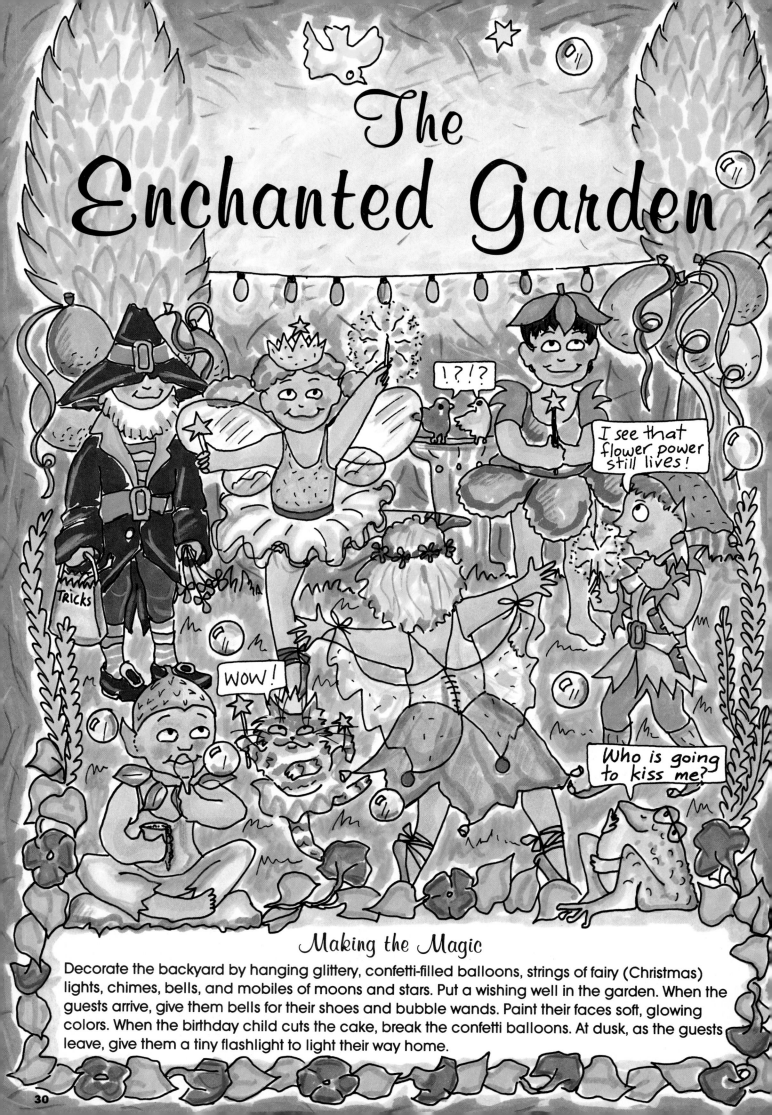

The Enchanted Garden

Making the Magic

Decorate the backyard by hanging glittery, confetti-filled balloons, strings of fairy (Christmas) lights, chimes, bells, and mobiles of moons and stars. Put a wishing well in the garden. When the guests arrive, give them bells for their shoes and bubble wands. Paint their faces soft, glowing colors. When the birthday child cuts the cake, break the confetti balloons. At dusk, as the guests leave, give them a tiny flashlight to light their way home.

Fairy Wear

Flower Fairies

Crepe-paper petal skirt, neck piece and hat worn over swimsuit; colored tights; ballet shoes; flowers in hair

Elves

Colored tights; night cap with bell; jacket with crepe paper collar and cuffs; belt with big buckle; pointed ears; long socks with bells stitched on toes; silver hammer; bamboo flute

Leprechauns

Big felt hat with buckle; false beard; jacket; belt with big buckle; striped socks; tights; shoes with buckles; bag of tricks; a shamrock to carry

Spirit Fairies

Ballet dress or old petticoat covered with netting or muslin and bells on hem; gauze or colored cellophane wings, sprinkle with glitter or attach sequins; wand; crown; ballet slippers; chimes

Pixies

Vest; tights; tight cap (bathing cap); pointed ears; bare feet; finger cymbals; necklace made of leaves

Invitation

All Fairy Folk are invited to the
Enchanted Garden

to celebrate _____'s _____ birthday

on _____ between _____

at _____

R.S.V.P. _____

Delicacies from The Dewdrop Inn

 Glue glitter around the edge of the invitations.

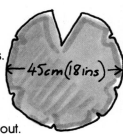 I could use a pair of extra wings.

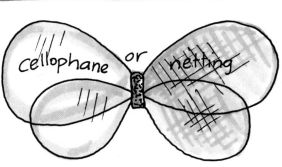 cellophane or netting

Fairy Wings

You will need: wire, wire snips, scissors, net or colored cellophane, glue, velcro (to attach to wings and dress), needle, thread, glitter, sequins, beads and stapler.

Wishing Well

Tape two sticks on either side of a plastic garbage can then staple the cardboard sign to top of sticks.

 WISHING WELL

Fairy Crown

head size

You will need: cardboard, glue, scissors, measuring tape, gold or silver paint, sequins, beads, glitter, stars, foil.

Lily Pads

You will need: green cardboard, pencil and scissors. Draw lily pads on pieces of cardboard big enough to sit and stand on, then cut out.

 45cm (18ins)

Use lily pads instead of chairs.

Games

The Bees' Knees

Blow up several long balloons. The children stand in a circle with some of them holding the balloons between their knees. While the music is playing the children with the balloons pass them on to the next child using only their knees. When the music stops the children with the balloons are out. Children who pop balloons are also out.

Green Frog

Divide the children into groups of elves, fairies, etc. Place enough chairs in a circle for all the children except one. This child is the Green Frog who stands in the middle and calls out a group. For example, if the Green Frog calls Elves, all the Elves must rush to change their seats while the Green Frog races to an empty seat. If the Green Frog does get a seat then he or she becomes one of the Elves and the child who misses out becomes the Green Frog.

Fish for a Wish

First make your wishing well (page 31), then fill it with a selection of small prizes such as silver stars, paper flowers, etc. Wrap the gifts in colored paper and attach a small magnet on the bottom. Provide each child in turn with a fishing rod that has a magnet attached to the end of the fishing line (string). The children then fish for a wish to take home with them. Alternatively, fill the wishing well with small gifts and the children may close their eyes and dip into the well with a cup or ladle.

Musical Lily Pads

Arrange the lily pads (page 31) in a circle with one lily pad less than the number of children. To the sound of music, the children jump from one pad to the next, and when the music stops, all children must be standing on a pad. The last child to reach a pad with another child on it, is out. Remove one pad, then restart the music. The game continues until there is only one pad left. The winner is the first child on to the last pad.

WISHING WELL

I wish for some catnip.

I wish they'd play leapfrog!

Spell-breaker:
Tie a balloon to each child's ankle. On the word "go" the children try to break each other's balloons. The last intact balloon is the winner.

The Dewdrop Inn Menu

Dainty Dip
Fairy Fingers page 45
Spell Salad
Pixie Pizzas page 45
Blossoms*
Lily Jell-O* with Lime Sherbert
Star Cookies* page 44
Moonshine*
Fairy Ring Cake* page 45
Bag of Tricks to take home

* see illustrations

IDEA — Put gummy frogs and snakes into each take-home bag.

Star Cookies

Make star cookies, ice with pink, green, and blue icing and decorate with silver sprinkles.

Spell Salad

Make a green salad, with cooked, star-shaped pasta.

Lily Jell-O

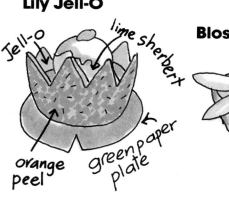

Jell-O · lime sherbert · orange peel · green paper plate

Blossoms

whipped cream · almonds · apricot halves

Fairy Ring Cake

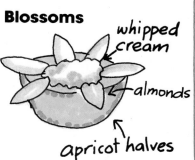

Pipe birthday greeting in icing. · Candy Cane · meringue

Moonshine

raspberry drink mix
lemonade
colored ice cubes

I could jump out of the middle of the cake!

HAPPY BIRTHDAY ALEX

SPACE STATION ZERO

Face Painting

Use face paints to make yourself look out of this world. Mix shades of green, blue, purple, silver and gold to exaggerate and outline your eyebrows, mouth and nose. Draw on scars and eyebrows or stick on glitter and stars.

Setting the Scene

Create a space-station atmosphere in your home with these decorations: black cloth with holes punched in it over windows; space mobile; painted paper plates for moon/planet mobiles; spray-painted ping pong balls; old TV set with snow on screen; fluorescent paint; strobe lights; colored lights; siren light; balloons and helium balloons; star mobiles; computer games; control panel; prerecorded tape of countdown, radio messages, static patterns.

Galactic Attire

(the more far out the better!)

- pillow case tunics
- rubber gloves sprayed silver or gold
- long gloves glued and glittered
- tights/leg warmers/colored pantihose/boots
- goggles/decorated sun glasses/ snow visor/sun visor
- portable radio or cassette player
- ear muffs
- ice cream container helmets/ bathing caps
- bike helmet/baseball cap
- aluminum foil jewelery/beads/ sequins/glitter/bottle tops
- cloaks
- ray guns*
- stick on silver and gold stars
- decorated gun holsters

* see illustration

ATTENTION

all galaxy travellers & aliens, Beam down to space station

_____

on the _____ between _____

to celebrate _____ th

year in the solar system.

Oxygen provided for earthlings.

RSVP _____

Space rations provided by Countdown Cafe.

Antennae Headpiece — springs, head band, ping pong balls

Reptile Alien — goggles, bathing cap, face paint

Circuit Belt — old belt, old transistor parts

Ray Gun — water pistol, paper cup, paper

Paper Plate Headpiece — paper plate, cut out to fit head, string

Space Mobile

You will need: a bicycle wheel, silver spray paint, rags, newspapers, string, glue, glitter, balloons, cardboard, space shapes and space "junk." Work in a ventilated space with a parent to help you.

Control Panel

You will need: large cardboard carton, toilet rolls, plastic tops for knobs, glue, paint, felt pens, strip drawings or magazine pictures, fantasy pictures, scissors, tape.

GAMES

Planet Tag

Place colored cardboard circles on the ground and write the name of a different planet on each. Choose two children to be taggers. On command, the other children must hop between the planets without being tagged. They can stop on each planet for a maximum of 10 seconds but after that, must move off. No more than three children are allowed on any one planet. When tagged, the child is eliminated. The game continues until only one child is left.

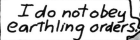

I do not obey earthling orders.

Memory Mode

Prepare two sets of cards with space words, such as satellite, orbit, Uranus, rocket, etc. written on them. Divide the children into two teams sitting facing each other. On the words, "Key In," the first child picks up the top card, reads it then passes it on to each child in the team to read. The last child puts it on the ground face down. Continue in this way until the whole pack has been read. On the instruction "Recall," each child in turn calls out as many words as they can remember. The team with the most correct words wins.

Astronaut Says

One child is the Astronaut and stands facing the other children. To play, the Astronaut acts out gestures and describes them, such as "Astronaut says, moon walk in slow motion." The others copy the Astronaut exactly. If the Astronaut gives any instructions without saying, "Astronaut says," the children must not follow them. If they do, they are out.

Space Race

Put a selection of 15-20 items on a tray. The children look at the items for 60 seconds and then write down as many articles as they can remember. They have a time limit of 30 seconds to write and the one with the most correct items written down by the end of the time limit is the winner.

Space Odyssey

One child starts a story by telling a few sentences such as "Once upon a time a young earthling catapulted from a burning space ship and landed on the planet Dripon." The next child continues the story, and so on around the circle. A parent could also take the role of storyteller.

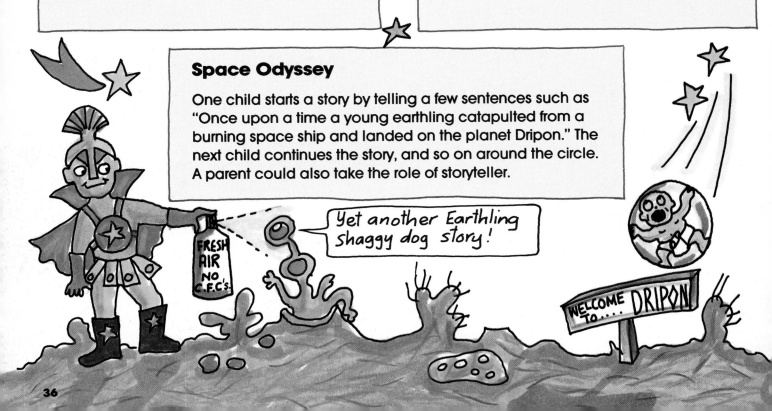

Yet another Earthling shaggy dog story!

FRESH AIR NO C.F.C's.

WELCOME TO.... DRIPON

Countdown Cafe Menu

Shuttle Spread page 44

Antenna

Aliens page 44

Sputniks *

Crater Cookies page 44

Saturn Salad with Satellite Dressing

Flying Saucers page 45

Orbit Ice Cream *

Rocket Fuel *

UFO Cake * page 46

Space rations to take home *

* see illustrations

Saturn Salad

Make a green salad, add hard-boiled egg yolks and cut egg whites into rings. Add carrot rings, cucumber rings, cheese rings, or any other ingredient that slices into circles or rings. Dress with green goddess or ranch dressing

Rocket Fuel

lime drink mix
7 Up or Sprite
ice cubes

Mix and serve with space-age straws.

Orbit Ice Cream

wafers

Space Rations

In small plastic bottles, such as a vitamin bottle, pack: jelly beans, M&Ms, and roasted nuts. Label bottle with child's name.

SPACE R
LYDIA

Sputniks

You will need: orange halves, cocktail picks, olives, cheese cubes, grapes, and pineapple pieces.

Place "alien" balloon in a fish bowl for a table decoration.

U.F.O. Cake

Decorate the cake plate with "space" motifs.

IDEA

Just get this off me before they cut the cake!

Making the Big Top

parent dressed as the Ring Master

tent-colored sheets over
  clothesline/beach umbrellas/
  camping tents

colored lights

crepe-paper bunting

balloons

stars and moons pinned on tent

flags, streamers, hooters

striped poles (wrap with crepe paper)

buckets for water, confetti, sawdust

tubs/tightrope/swing

lemonade and popcorn stall

hot dog stand

ring of decorated stools and seats

trestle tables

fortune-telling booth

hoops to jump through

disposable tablecloth

water pistols

music for Grand Parade

plastic bowling pins

ticket books

tin-can stilts

* see illustrations

STEP RIGHT UP!

The Big Top has come to town to
celebrate _____'s ___ th birthday

Dress as a clown, strong man, tightrope
walker or any other circus performer
and join the Grand Parade starting
at _____ until _____

Don't forget your ticket book for free
drinks, fun, and games.
Eats at The Big Top Barbecue.
RSVP _____

Color in the invitations.

THE GRAND PARADE

Clowns

Baggy clothes or clothes that are too small, braces, floppy bow, old boots with flapping soles, bowler hat/top hat, red wig (string or red wool threaded through bathing cap), red nose (page 41), gloves, ruffles, stilts, water pistols

Lion Tamer

Safari suit and pith helmet, or loose white shirt, jodhpurs (baggy pants tucked into boots), sash tied around the waist, gloves, boots, medallion, whip, scars, a brave face

Human Cannonball

Greased body, crash helmet, leotard, vest with lightning flash, elbow and knee pads, boots with wings attached, bruises, parachute or umbrella

Bareback Rider/ Trapeze Artist

Ballet dress, swimsuit with net skirt, spangles/ sequins/glitter, tights, bare feet, ballet slippers, plumed headwear, bikini top, wrist straps

Fire Eater

Cloak, tights, sash, gloves, rag-wrapped sticks, bottle of water marked "Fire Water"

Elephant Trainer

Turban, brooch, silk dressing gown, sash, baggy pants, slippers, elephant prodder

Strong Man

Vest, big belt, tights, swim-suit, striped socks, balloon weights, medallion, mustache, chains, tattoos, high tops

Acrobat/Jugglers

Flared satin pants, silver braid, bolero vest, spangles, colored balls, plastic bowling pins, wrist straps

Ticket Book

You will need: pieces of colored card approximately 7 x 3cm (3 x 1½in), scissors, pen, stapler, stars

Admit one to Bonnie's BIG TOP PARTY

Free Face Paint

lemonade and popcorn for one

Admit one to Magic Show

Admit one to Bonnie's BIG TOP PARTY

Send ticket books out with the invitations.

Just show me the ropes.

Once upon a time in deepest, darkest Africa....

I feel a little stilted!

Pssst, take me with you please.

PAINT

To Make...

Clown's Nose

You will need: an old egg carton, red paint, string, scissors. Cut out the sections of an egg carton and paint them red. Put a hole in each side, thread with string and tie behind the head.

Bean Bags

Sew up two cloth squares, leaving a gap for filling. Fill bags half full with dried beans or peas, then sew up the hole. You can also use socks.

Bowling Pins

Paint plastic bottles with stripes, dots and stars in bold colors, then partly fill with sand or pebbles.

Paint-Can Stilts

Clean two 4 lt (1 gal) cans. Put two holes in the bottom, placed either side of your foot. Thread a piece of rope through to make a strap and secure with knots. Paint with bold patterns.

Face Painting

Tiger

Liontamer & Strongman

Sad Clown

Happy Clown

You will need: cold cream, tissues, powder, face paints, eyebrow pencils, eyeshadow, glitter, a mirror and an old towel.

Ask your local drugstore if they have any make up samples.

IDEA

I'm all fired up!

FIRE WATER

One more crash landing and I'm quitting!

Just another view of life!

41

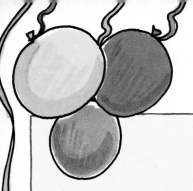

GAMES

Tightrope Walk

Secure a thick rope or wooden plank about 15cm (6in) above the ground and have children walk along it. The ones who reach the other end can then return, doing simple tricks, such as dipping their foot below the rope as they take each step. The child who crosses the rope the most times is the winner.

Elephant's Tail

Draw an elephant on a large sheet of paper and mark an X where its tail should be. Color and cut out a tail. Each child in turn wears a blindfold, spins around three times and tries to pin the tail on the elephant. The child who pins the tail closest is the winner.

Well just how would you feel?

Ring Master Says

The Ring Master calls out and mimes an action, such as "Ring Master says wash the elephant." The other circus members then also mime washing the elephant. However, if the Ring Master doesn't say "Ring Master says" before giving a command and the children follow the mime, they are out. The last child left becomes the new Ring Master.

Bowling

Paint some 2-liter plastic bottles and fill them with a little sand to use as pins. Line them up and use a tennis ball to bowl them over. Write different numbers on each pin and keep score of how many each child bowls over.

Clown Workshop

Children design their own clown makeup which another child applies. They can then work out a clown routine in pairs and perform for the rest of the group. The Ring Master can assist the fun by holding up cards for the audience that say, Laugh! Cry! Cheer!

Sack Race

Hold relay races in which the children put their feet in old pillow cases or gunny sacks and jump to the other end of the room or yard. The fastest team of jumpers wins.

Give each child a score card and pencil to add up the grand score.

Set up a penny arcade with side-show games using simple props.

Hook Board
Ring Fling
Card Flick
Hot Shot

BIG TOP BARBECUE

Drum Roll Dip page 45
Lion Burgers *
Hot Dogs
Chicken Drumsticks page 44
Sawdust Salad
Clown Cookies * page 44
Monkey Business page 44
Popcorn
Ice Cream
Lemonade
Big Top Cake * page 45
Carmel Apples to take home *

* see illustrations

Lion Burgers

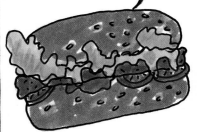

You will need: sesame buns, lettuce, cheese, tomato slices, ketchup, mayonnaise, ground beef patty.

Carmel Apples

Write guest's name on stick.

Clown Cookies

jellybean
coconut
Cherry
icing
licorice

Lemonade

You will need: soda water, lemon juice, sugar, freshly chopped mint, ice cubes. Mix before serving.

BIG TOP CAKE

TOBY

Where is the fire?

I just want to go home!

Basic Recipes

Green Lagoon/Dinosaur Dip/
Shuttle Spread
Serves: 8-10

1 clove garlic (optional)
2 medium-sized ripe avocados, peeled
200 ml (7 fl oz or ⅔ cup) natural yogurt
salt and pepper
lemon juice, to taste
chili sauce, to taste

Squeeze the garlic into a dish, then add the avocados. Mash with a fork until smooth, then add the yogurt. Season to taste with the salt and pepper, lemon juice and chili sauce. Serve with corn chips or carrot and celery sticks.

Note: The lemon juice prevents the avocado from going brown so the dish can be made several hours before the party.

Fish Cookies/Clown Cookies/
Clue Cookies/Skull Cookies/
Star Cookies
Makes: 30-35

150 g (5 oz or 12 tablespoons) unsalted butter
75 g (3 oz or 1/3 cup) confectioner's sugar
2 egg yolks
vanilla extract, to taste
175 g (6 oz or 1½ cups) all purpose flour
¼ teaspoon salt

Cream the butter and sugar until white, then add the egg yolks and vanilla extract, beating well. Sift in the flour and salt, and mix to make a light, soft dough. Roll out thinly on a floured surface and cut into desired shapes. Bake in an oven preheated to 150°C (300°F, Mark 2) for 10-15 minutes or until golden brown. Cool, then ice.

Batwings/Pterodactyl Wings/Aliens/
Chicken Drumsticks
Serves: 8-10

finely grated orange peel and juice of 1 orange
1 clove garlic, crushed (optional)
3 tablespoons honey
2 tablespoons mustard
1.4 kg (3 lb) chicken drumsticks or chicken wings

Mix the orange peel and juice together with the garlic. Combine the honey and mustard, and stir it into the marinade. Pour the marinade over the chicken and turn until well coated. Leave to marinate overnight.

Put the drumsticks/wings in a single layer in a baking dish and bake in the marinade in an oven preheated to 180°C (350°F, Mark 4) for 15 minutes for the wings, and 25 minutes for the drumsticks. Turn the legs several times during cooking. To see if they are cooked, pierce the thickest part of the leg/wing with a skewer. It is cooked if the juices run clear. Cool completely, then store in the refrigerator until required. This recipe can be made two days ahead.

Note: If preparing this recipe for the barbecue, precook the day before as above, then reheat on the barbecue, brushing with the marinade.

Monkey Business/Trog's Toenails
Makes: 20

250 g (9 oz or 1 cup + 1 tablespoon) butter
125 g (4 oz or 4 squares) dark chocolate
400 g (14 oz or 2¹/₃ cups) sugar
3 eggs
¼ teaspoon salt
1 teaspoon vanilla extract
125 g (4 oz or 1 cup) all purpose flour
125 g (4 oz or ½ cup) unsalted roasted peanuts

Melt the butter over gentle heat, then add the chocolate. Beat the sugar, eggs, salt and vanilla, pour the chocolate and butter over, and mix well. Sift the flour over and gently fold in with the peanuts, until well blended. Pour into a 34 x 27 cm (13 x 10 in) greased and floured tray. Bake in an oven preheated to 180°C (350°F, Mark 4) for 40 minutes or until a skewer inserted comes out clean. The slice should be crunchy on the outside and fudgy in the middle.

Barbecued Diptrodon Ribs
Serves: 8

1.8 kg (4 lb) pork spareribs, separated

Marinade

2 tablespoons soy sauce
1 tablespoon red wine vinegar
2 cloves garlic, crushed (optional)
1 tablespoon tomato ketchup
1 teaspoon sesame oil
½ tablespoon honey
salt and pepper
2 tablespoons vegetable oil

Two days before the party, combine all the marinade ingredients in a large shallow dish, add the spareribs and turn until well coated. Leave, covered with plastic wrap, to marinate for 24 hours, turning occasionally.

The day before, precook in an oven heated to 180°C (350°F, Mark 4) for 45 minutes, turning occasionally. Cool, then store, covered, in the refrigerator. Barbecue over hot coals for 10 minutes, basting frequently.

Note: If you are not planning a barbecue, finish cooking the ribs under the broiler and serve hot or cold.

Rock Cakes/Crater Cookies
Makes: 20

175 g (6 oz or ¾ cup) butter or margarine
150 g (5 oz or ⅔ cup) sugar
150 g (5 oz or ⅔ cup) brown sugar
2 eggs
375 g (13 oz or 3¼ cups) all purpose flour
1½ teaspoons baking soda
½ teaspoon salt
250 g (9 oz or 1⅓ cups) chocolate chips
1 teaspoon vanilla

Cream the butter and sugar, then beat in the eggs. Sift in the flour, soda and salt. Mix in the chocolate chips and vanilla. Spoon egg-sized mounds onto a greased tray and bake in an oven preheated to 180°C (350°F, Mark 4) for 30 minutes or until cooked.

Fossil Fudge/Furtive Fudge
Makes: 30 squares

450 g (1 lb or 2 cups) granulated sugar
75 g (3 oz or 6 tablespoons) butter or margarine
150 ml (¼ pt or ⅔ cup) milk
175 g (6 oz) can evaporated milk
½ teaspoon vanilla extract

Put the sugar, butter, milk and evaporated milk into a heavy-based pan and heat gently, stirring constantly until dissolved. Stop stirring and allow mixture to come to a boil, then continue boiling, stirring occasionally, until the mixture reaches 116°C (240°F).

Remove pan from the heat and add the vanilla. Beat the mixture with a wooden spoon until it becomes thick and grainy. Pour into a lightly oiled 18 cm (7 in) shallow tin and leave for 5-10 minutes or until almost set. Cut the soft fudge into squares with a sharp knife, then leave until cold before cutting out the pieces. The fudge can be made up to two weeks ahead and stored in an airtight container.

Note: Add cocoa to make chocolate-flavored fudge.

Undercover Pizza/Pixie Pizzas/
Flying Saucers

pizza crust mix
pizza sauce
mozarella cheese
your favorite toppings (choose from pepperoni, sausage, Canadian bacon, olives, tomatoes, onions, pineapple, green pepper, mushrooms)

Follow the instructions on the mix package, prepare the dough for the crust. Add sauce, cheese, and toppings. Bake as instructed on the package.

Antennae/Dem Bones/Coral Reefs/
Fairy Fingers
Makes: 20-40

50 g (2 oz or 1 cup) cheese, grated
2 sheets puff pastry
1 egg, beaten
paprika

For **Antennae**, sprinkle the cheese on one sheet of puff pastry, then cover with other sheet. Press together to seal, then cut into narrow strips, rolling slightly to seal edges. Brush with beaten egg, dust with paprika.

For **Dem Bones**, cut pastry into bone shapes, gently roll to seal edges, brush with beaten egg and sprinkle with paprika.

For **Coral Reefs**, cut pastry into coral shapes. Sprinkle with grated cheese and paprika.

For **Fairy Fingers**, cut pastry into fingers, brush with beaten egg and decorate with sugar sprinkles. Bake all shapes in an oven preheated to 220°C (425°F, Mark 7) for 5-10 minutes or until puffed and golden.

White with Fright Dip/Devious Dip/
Drum Roll Dip

French onion soup mix
1 cup sour cream

Mix half a packed of French onion soup mix with one cup of sour cream. Mix and chill.

Basic Birthday Cake

175 g (6 oz or ¾ cup) butter
175 g (6 oz or ¾ cup) sugar
1 tablespoon corn syrup
4 eggs
350 g (12 oz/3 cups) all purpose flour
1½ teaspoons baking powder
1 tablespoon cornstarch
180 ml (6½ fl oz) milk

Cream the butter, sugar and Golden Syrup, then add the eggs one at a time, beating well after each addition. Sift the flour and baking powder together and mix the cornstarch and milk. Fold in the flour adding it alternatively with the milk.

Pour into a greased and floured 20 cm (8 in) baking tin and bake in an oven preheated to 180°C (350°F, Mark 4) oven for 50-60 minutes or until a toothpick inserted into the center comes out clean.

Fairy Ring Cake

Prepare as for the previous recipe, Basic Birthday Cake, then divide the mixture into three equal portions. Add a couple of drops of red food coloring to one, 1 tablespoon of cocoa to another and leave the third plain. Spoon, in alternate spoonfuls, into a prepared 20 cm (8 in) ring tin. Bake for 50-60 minutes in an oven preheated to 180°C (350°F, Mark 4).

When cool, ice with green icing and decorate with sugar sprinkles. Make toadstools with meringues and candy canes, dotting the tops with red icing. Set toadstools on the cake with a candle in each. Decorate the serving plate with paper or silk flowers and leaves.

Big Top Cake

Prepare the Basic Birthday Cake mixture and divide into three parts. Color one part with a couple of drops of red food coloring, one with 1 tablespoon cocoa and leave the third plain. Spoon in layers into a 20 cm (8 in) round cake tin. Bake in an oven preheated to 180°C (350°F, Mark 4) oven for 50-60 minutes.

When cold, decorate with plain icing and make a circus ring in the center with yellow-colored coconut. Place plastic circus animals in the middle and pink marshmallows around the perimeter with a candle in each one. Pipe striped icing on side of cake and decorate with candy stars. Fly the child's name from a bright plastic drinking straw placed in the center.

Gigantosaurus Cake

Make double the Basic Birthday Cake mix, add 175 g (6 oz) chocolate chips, divide in half and bake in two greased and floured 20 cm (8 in) square cake tins for

50-60 minutes or until a skewer inserted into the center comes out clean.

When cold, sandwich together with whipped cream mixed with nuts and chocolate chips. Ice with a pale colored icing and decorate with plastic dinosaurs, and footprints made from icing. Put candles in rock-like candies.

Basic Chocolate Cake

125 g (4 oz or ½ cup) butter
125 g (4 oz or ½ cup) sugar
1 tablespoon corn syrup
3 eggs
175 g (6 oz or 1½ cups) all purpose flour
1½ tablespoons cocoa
1½ teaspoons baking soda
250 ml (9 fl oz) milk

Cream the butter, sugar and corn syrup. Add the eggs, one at a time, beating well after each addition. Sift the flour and cocoa into the butter mixture, alternating with the combined soda and milk. Pour into a 20 cm (8 in) greased and floured baking tin and bake in an oven preheated to 180°C (350°F, Mark 4) oven for 45-50 minutes or until a toothpick inserted into the center comes out clean.

Island Cake/Bomb Cake

Make double the Basic Chocolate Cake mixture and pour half into a 20 cm (8 in) greased and floured baking tin. Pour the remaining half into a 15 cm (6 in) diameter basin. Bake in an oven preheated to 180°C (350°F, Mark 4) for 45-50 minutes (60 minutes for the basin) or until a toothpick inserted into the center comes out clean.

For the Island Cake: when cold, trim both cakes so they are level, then ice together. Ice the island peak with green icing and the beach with yellow. Pour blue Jell-O into a suitable shallow tray (approx. 30 cm/12 in) and leave until set. Place the cake in the center and sprinkle yellow and orange jelly beans or M&Ms around the base for beach, set in gummy fish. Cut licorice strips into triangles and set into Jell-O. Put candles, trimmed with green foil, around perimeter and place a plastic drinking straw in the center with a name flag attached.

For the Bomb Cake: Ice cakes together with chocolate icing. Sprinkle over silver sparkles. Pipe decoration around base of cake. Place a long thin red candle in the center to represent a fuse.

Cobweb Cake

Make Basic Chocolate Cake mixture, folding in chopped white marshmallows. Pour into a greased and floured 20 cm (8 in) round tin and bake in an oven preheated to 180°C (350°F, Mark 4) for 45-50 minutes. When cold, ice with chocolate icing and pipe on a white spider's web. Place a black toy spider in the center. Place marshmallows, studded with black jelly beans, around the edge with candles in the middle.

U.F.O. Cake

Make the Basic Chocolate Cake mixture and pour into a floured and greased 20 cm (8 in) round cake pan. Put 4 tablespoons of batter into a shallow metal basin. Bake in an oven preheated to 180°C (350°F, Mark 4) for 45-50 minutes or until a toothpick comes out clean. The basin will only take about 15 minutes to bake and will need checking regularly.

Allow cakes to cool on a rack, then ice the cakes together. Make up a batch of white icing and divide it into three, coloring two sections of it. Ice the cake, swirling the colors, then decorate with marshmallows around the edge and Lifesavers for portholes. In the center, put three drinking straws, with maraschino cherries on top, place candles around the edge.

Suggested Materials to Collect and Use

paper bags
brown wrapping paper
used wrapping paper
old Christmas and birthday cards
newspapers
pegs
paper
cardboard scraps
wallpaper scraps
paper doilies

egg cartons
ice-cream containers
yogurt containers
cardboard rolls
pipe cleaners
paper plates
styrofoam containers
styrofoam balls
old magazines
felt

plastic bottles
old pantihose
margarine containers
tissue and shoe boxes
thin and thick string
wool
beads and buttons
modeling clay

Suggested Materials to Buy

crepe paper
colored tissue paper
cellophane paper
sheets of thin, colored cardboard

gummed paper
colored stars
sparkles
cotton wool

face paints
colored hair sprays

Equipment

scissors
pencils
colored pencils
paints
erasers

glue
felt-tipped pens
paper clips
elastic bands
pinking shears

stapler
needle and thread
hole punch
elastic
sticky tape

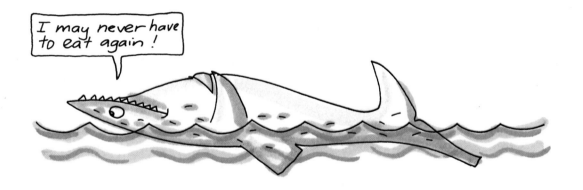